Waiting
on
My Release

From the Ashes
of Negative Thinking

David Fowler : Redbloodink

WESTBOW
PRESS®
A DIVISION OF THOMAS NELSON
& ZONDERVAN

WestBow Press books may be ordered through booksellers or by contacting:

WestBow Press
A Division of Thomas Nelson & Zondervan
1663 Liberty Drive
Bloomington, IN 47403
www.westbowpress.com
1 (866) 928-1240

ISBN: 978-1-9736-0790-8 (sc)
ISBN: 978-1-9736-0791-5 (e)

Library of Congress Control Number: 2017917641

Print information available on the last page.

WestBow Press rev. date: 2/13/2018

Dedication

I dedicate this book to Debra Kay Shew for she inspired me to finish writing the self help book. I love you Miss Debbie more than my words could ever express thank you for inspiring me to keep going through this long process and accomplishment.

Waiting on My Release

Chapter One

There I laid entombed in my own grave clothes. Gave clothes of self-regret, remorse, anxiety, hate and torment over how I had treated others and myself. I was reading the Holy Bible to pass the time trying to figure out what life really means. I was truly lost in my crimes and transgressions against others and myself. I had been living a living death and had no idea that my drug and alcohol addictions were keeping me in a Hades of my own creation. I thought I was worthless, unsaveable, unreachable and incapable of having a successful life.

Days had gone by as I read the Bible, I was trying to understand what the words were supposed to be teaching me. In these days of being self-absorbed in my own little world, I kept noticing this older man sitting off in a corner by himself in the overcrowded dorm. His hands usually folded in a prayer like manner, staring off like if he was somewhere else in life.

I always tried to pay no attention to him or anyone else for that matter, I found myself in a place I would rather have not been in anyways. I was homeless and went into an abandon church to seek shelter from the cold, windy, rainy day. I thought it was a great idea to take refuge there in that small town left behind church, looking like it was left for ruins like myself. In that old run-down church I found hardly anything of use to me, then I saw a stairway leading up to its second story that was in just as bad shape. There was a hallway with several rooms off to each side of it, I picked one of the rooms to sit in too eat my lunch. I had just pulled the lunch out of a supermarket dumpster just a few blocks away from the church.

The lunch consisted of some shrimp that had been precooked and shrimp sauce. The shrimp and sauce were still cold and packaged, so I knew it was safe to eat. Even though the sour smell of garbage lingered in the air from the container, the smell still bothered me even though the experience wasn't new to me. I had been living on the streets for several months before that day in the church. I had eaten a couple of the shrimp and took a good swig of the beer someone had given just before my dumpster dive.

Just about that time I heard a great commotion of noise coming from down stairs. Unsure of what was happening I tried to hide myself, I found no-where to hide so I just laid down hoping for the best. The noises started to get closer to me so I closed my eyes like if I was asleep. Just then the door to the room I was in got kicked in by a few people that identified themselves as the city police department. I then opened my eyes to look up and see it was true, there stood four police officers surrounding me like I was a hardened criminal trying to rob a bank. They pulled me off the floor like an old rag doll and they took me down the hallway proceeding to charge me with trespassing, burglary, burglary tools and petty theft. I begged them to only trespass me since I was homeless and I was just trying to avoid the blustery winter day. The officers looked at me with disbelief and disgust on their faces, with the comments of look at what you have done to this church.

I will have to admit the church was in ruins but I had only been there for fifteen minutes before the police showed up. No matter what I said to them about how long I had been there or that I hadn't been there before, they still insisted that I had done all that great damage to the church. The police then walked me down the stairs back through the churches sanctuary and out the front doors that were broke and unlockable when I showed up in the first place. That's why I didn't understand the burglary charges the police had given me to begin with. As all this was running through my brain while laying there in my bunk, I felt like the older man was calling to me.

Chapter Two

The days went on as I read my Bible in the mix of all the loud noise and confusion of everyone trying to out talk everyone else. Never mind the noise of the television and loud speakers as inmates names were being called out for various reasons. At times it was hard to concentrate on what I was reading never mind understanding what I was reading. The old man would catch my attention at times as I watched him walk around the dorm, when he wasn't sitting in his usual spot starring off like if he wasn't even there.

Thirty days had gone by now and I just knew I wasn't going to be released. I just had a great feeling that my life was heading for a new beginning, how true that feeling became three days later in the inside court room of the county jail. The line of inmates ahead of me started to go before the judge one by one to find out their fate. Inmate after inmate the judge would seal their fate, some were released some were held for another court date and others were sent off to drug and alcohol programs.

My nerves started to jump as I saw my turn getting closer and closer to stand up on that podium. Finally my turn was next and my heart felt like it fell into my stomach. My name was called so I stood up and made my way slowly to the podium and there I stood with my knees trembling like when I was a child waiting for my punishment from my parents. The judge spoke to the states attorney, the states attorney started to reply but just then their computers shut down. The only thing left that could be done was for me to wait for the corrections officers to take me back to my dorm after court was over.

Nothing happens in the blinking of an eye or the snapping of the fingers, it seemed like it took hours as the time passed by slowly for me. I was finally escorted back to my dorm by the jails correction officers. Even though you're in jail behind walls and locked doors inmates are not allowed to wonder down the hallways alone. The correction officers lead us back to our dorms in groups stopping off at holding cells near other cell blocks split into four dorms.

We finally made it back to my cell block and I felt so grateful, I don't know if it was because I was released from the hand cuffs, shackles and chains or I was back in a place I had become so familiar with. Now back inside the dorm I had gotten so use to within the last thirty three days of my life, I saw many of the same faces and a few new ones. My heart started to race as I looked around the dorm, just then I saw the older man sitting off in a different spot with his hands folded like usual. My heart slowed to a steadier of a beat, I'm not sure if it was because of the older man's peaceful demeanor of if it was I thought of his safety. He was among all of these strong young men that could erupt into a violent state of action in minutes. I moved quickly back through the dorm back to my bunk to find my Bible under my pillow where I had placed it. I laid back down on my bunk with Bible in hand, the pages flipped open and stopped in the New Testament and to this day I'm still not sure where. By now it was well pass lunch time and making its way towards the dinner hour. Other than the few new faces everything seemed the same to me. I kept reading my Bible trying to understand the best I could.

I believe I skipped dinner on this night with my stomach upset, I just couldn't believe these false charges had stuck and I was still in jail. I had been praying all of these days for my release and just like before my prayers were unanswered. I understand now my prayers were being answered but just not the way I wanted or understood. The next morning came as chow time was being called out over the loud speakers. I got off my bunk and headed for the line I was hungry and needed the food. With my stomach in knots I sat down to eat, even though I had a hard time eating my food I forced it down with every swallow. The day seemed to be going like the other thirty three days before I looked around the dorm as always just to check out my environment. To my surprise I didn't see the peaceful looking old man, I just though to myself " well I guess he got released." I reached under my make-shift pillow grabbed my Bible and started to read.

Now in this over-crowded dorm I became known as Christian, and I'm still not sure why to this day. I spent a few hours reading and lunch was called out over the loud speakers like all the days before. Chow, chow time as always and a line began to form with a bunch of pushing, shoving and yelling as lunch bags and juices were handed through the slot in the dorm door. Like always after chow I took my place on my bunk and reached under my pillow and grabbed my Bible. I let the pages flip open and stopped where they may. I started reading trying to block out all the rowdy noise that bounced off the four block walls.

Chapter Three

That evening after chow call and the dorm settled down I heard my name called over the loud speakers. They said "Fowler pack it up," but I knew I wasn't going home, well not home but back to the streets that I had been so familiar with. I went to the door with my laundry basket full of my stuff which consisted of my blanket, change of uniform, tooth brush, tooth paste and the Bible of course this was all county issued to every inmate. I wasn't hand-cuffed or shackled this time I was just escorted to a new cell block. I found myself transferred to a dorm where they kept a trusty. A trusty is an inmate who they would deem good enough to work in the jail. Trusty jobs varied from the kitchen, halls, booking (where they took in new inmates to be processed) and whatever else the jail needed help for it to run as smooth as possible. The correction officer's main job was to keep order and make head counts to make sure no one escaped, the rest of the jail was left up to the inmates to take care of.

I walked my way into my new dorm to find myself on the day room floor again. The day room floor is the main part of the dorm for the inmates' social time during the day. I found my bunk and sat down in a sigh of relief, I looked around briefly just too check out the crowd. I couldn't believe my eyes as I looked far off in one of the corners there sat the older man with his hands folded like always starring off like if he wasn't even there in that cold loud environment. I grabbed my Bible out of my laundry basket and laid back on my bunk. I didn't feel much like reading so I just laid it on my chest. Lock down came around at ten o' clock P.M. That's when all the inmates have to go to their cells for the night. Those of us on the day room floor just had to stay on our bunks unless we had to use the bathroom, our bathroom was an empty cell on the bottom floor.

The next morning seemed to come fast as chow, chow time came over the loud speakers. I got up and headed for the chow line that was more tamed since we were trusties, trusties have to act more civilized because of our responsibilities of helping run the jail. After chow like always I went back to my bunk to read my Bible, I guess some of it was making sense to me because I was raised in a family that went to church every Sunday. I had just laid back on my bunk with my Bible and let the pages roll open like always. This time I felt like if someone was staring at me. I took the Bible down from in front of my face to find it was true, about twenty feet away the older man was staring at me intently.. I still couldn't really see what he looked like at this time because I never got a real close look at him. He seemed to stand over six feet tall and appeared to weigh at least two hundred pounds from what I could tell. He smiled at me as if to say a gentle hello, I smiled back but my smile might have been a little less sincere than his. He turned and walked away to make his trips around the dorm like I had seen him do so many times before. I didn't try to mingle with the crowd so no one bothered me as I would just sit and read my Bible.

I felt relaxed and comfortable in my new dorm, it wasn't anymore quiet then the dorm I was in before. I guess the dorm was a little more subdued because no one wanted to lose their job. Trusties have a little more freedom because they get to leave their dorms to work. So there I was reading my Bible, like always just trying to stay to myself. In my first dorm some of the inmates were reading the Bible it just seemed like the inmates that did would only read intermittently. I remembered as a child the Bible was referred to as the book of life. Having nothing else to do being stuck in this jail, I just wanted to understand something other then what I had already learned in life.

My earthly father had taught me about work and work ethics, he always told me if you ever want to get anywhere in life I would have to really apply myself. I wouldn't just have to apply myself but I would have to go above and beyond in all I did. He was a little hard on me at times as he tried to teach me how to be a finish carpenter. I gave up on him and the trade he was trying to teach me way to soon. The past is gone and now it's dead so I buried it where it lays in the past.

So there I was in my present in a jail. I now know today it was the place I needed to be reading the Bible and trying to figure out life and my life. Once again my Bible reading was interrupted by the loud speaker, chow, chow time this was a call for lunch. I got in line like always just to receive my bag and half cold juice. I became grateful for the food as I would just go off and eat by myself and eat.

Just then it happened the meeting that the older man or myself had been longing for. There he stood towering over me as I sat on the cold hard concrete floor in a corner. Now up close to me I could see he was over six feet tall and weighed more then two hindered pounds. He had longer hair and a beard with a wrinkling face. Smiling down at me with his soft twinkling eyes he said "hello my name is Paul." I looked back up at him with my trembling voice to say hello. I started to tell him my name, he interrupted me by saying "David it's so nice and pleasant to meet you." He then proceeded to say "I know what you're thinking how do I know your name." I stuttered a little bit as I responded yes to his statement. He then proceeded to tell me that no one's name could be a mystery in here like, unlike the outside. All you had to do is inquire a little bit and you could find out an inmate's name. The correction officers were not allowed to tell anyone what you had done to get yourself in there but your name wasn't a big issue. I sighed with a big relief as I said thank you. Then the old man asked me why I had thanked him. I proceeded to tell him that I was thinking I was sitting before God since he had known my name before I could respond.

The old man just chuckled at my statement so loud that it boomed through the dorm. I believe it was so loud and soothing that the dorm went silent for a moment in time. He then responded that he believed one day all of us as a human race were going to go before God upon our deaths. With this statement He also said that we all have a soul that belongs to God and that He loves us. I had a question for the old man since he seemed so wise. I never got the question out because he had excused himself from my presence to walk around the dorm like he always did. I proceeded to eat my lunch and headed back to my bunk like I had done so many days before. I took out my Bible from under my pillow and once again let it roll out to a page. I took it into hand and laid back on my bunk, to my surprise my Bible had opened to the book of Romans chapter one. I looked down to read and the first word I saw was the name Paul. Now I knew in my heart, head and thoughts this was not the Paul I had just met. It was very odd to me because my experience I just had and the old man did appear to be wise. Paul of the Holy Bible an Apostle of Jesus Christ had been dead for thousands of years. So I put all of these thoughts out of my head because I knew it was just coincidental that all this had just happened. So I just kept reading as the day went on because I wanted a peace of mind.

Over the loud speaker once again chow, chow time was called out, my stomach grumbling anyways I knew dinner was about to be served. I got up and went to the line and as I stood there I felt some kinda peacefulness. I normally wouldn't have turned to look behind me but I did, there he stood Paul towering over me by a few inches. I finally noticed his grayish eyes with that soft little twinkle in them. I didn't know why and still don't know why this old man had taken to me. He smiled and said hello, and this time my smile must have been sincere. Even though I didn't say hello or have time to say hello, I guess my smile said it for me. The old man or Paul I should say, asked me to move up because the line had moved. I finally made it to the door to receive my dinner making my way to my bunk I sat down to eat.

The jail was equipped with metal tables and benches but I didn't like to sit at them. Most of the time the tables seemed crowded and not only that everyone would be talking, and growing up sitting at my parent's dining-room table we were not to talk but eat. So I liked to sit by myself and just eat in my own silence, just then Paul showed up at my bunk side asking if he could sit with me. Not to be rude I said yes, so he sat down beside me and began to eat his dinner. I finally got up the nerve to ask him a question, I asked Paul why did he go out of his way to talk to me. He responded by saying "I have been watching you all of this time while we had been in jail." This caught me off guard a little and I figure Paul knew it by my facial expressions. Paul said "I am sorry I didn't mean watching you as if

I was stalking you, I just meant I noticed that you were reading the Bible so much it caught my attention." I then asked Paul why me reading the Bible would catch his attention so much. He responded " you see David many people in here or on the outside read the Bible but they lack the study of it." I responded by saying " really what's the difference? " At this time Paul just laughed at me in that deep booming sound like before. Once again I believe the dorm went silent like if it calmed everyone with joy and peace.

Paul then told me he would elaborate on his statement of the difference of just reading something or studying something, Paul seemed to not want to talk but eat instead. We sat there side by side in our own silence with the noise and confusion all around us, Paul seemed to eat his food in a hurry. Since he was finished with his dinner before me, he stood up and excused himself politely. I finished my dinner and got up to put my tray away. I went back to my bunk to do what I usually did, yes I grabbed my Bible from under my pillow where I kept it, like always I let the pages roll open to where they may. I started to read as all the noise and chaos drifted into the back- ground, as the words seemed to be jumping out at me now with more meaning. I stopped for a minute to think about what Paul had said to me earlier. People either read or study what they are reading, these words kept ringing through my mind so I shut my Bible and went to sleep. I woke up a few hours later to the loud speakers announcing lock down.

Chapter Four

The next morning like all the other days came with the announcement of chow time, so I made my way to the breakfast line. It seemed to be going slow on this morning as I waited my turn. I took my tray and headed to my bunk to sit, Paul once again showed up to ask if he could sit with me. I told him to take a seat that I didn't mind, there we were just like two old friends eating and talking. Paul turned his head to me and asked "did you think about what I said?" I responded with a yes. He asked me what I thought the difference was between reading and studying something. My answer was brief as I told him to study something a person should read the material over and over again until they understood it to the fullest of their capabilities. Paul looked at me with wide smiling eyes with a smile on his face to match. He began to speak to me like my father would have, son I just knew you had some smarts about you. He then asked me a question, "do you know what this scripture means?" Who so ever compels you to go with them one mile go another. I looked at the old man, straight into those grey eyes. (I bet with a lost look in my eyes.) I said to him," I guess if your friend wants to go somewhere you should go with them and maybe walk a little more if you don't want to.

Paul just chuckled at me this time softly so it wasn't heard by everyone. Paul turned to me and said my friend, the Bible is more than just a guide for our relationship with God, our family and friends. It applies to all of life as the speaker of those words were trying to tell us. I must of had a stupid look on my face as I spoke my words to him when I said. " Who was the speaker of those words Paul?" Paul's' answer came quickly and swiftly, " Jesus of course the wisest man who ever walked this planet." There was silence for a few moments between Paul and myself. I broke the silence with this statement, " Paul what made Him the wisest Man to ever walk this planet? " The old man just laughed at me, this time it just boomed through the dorm like the two times before.

Then he responded by saying " Jesus was the Word of God manifested into flesh and bone." He then went on to say " so the Word of God came into the world as a Man and in all my studies I found Jesus to be God in the flesh." There was silence for a minute or so this time before I broke it. Paul so you are telling me God came to earth to die! Paul answered me quickly with the word, " exactly. " My mind wouldn't stop thinking real fast so I spit it out the question, " why would God come here to die?" Paul piped up quickly and said, " look my son God was watching mankind from the beginning and found fault of how we were living." Our sacrifices of animals and whatever we thought would satisfy God was wrong. So I believe God came down to His creation to show us how to love Him, each other and ourselves the way He really wanted it from the beginning. I piped up and said, " Paul but if God died here on earth why does His Word say He lives forever?" Paul answered me by saying, " oh my silly child Jesus arose from the dead to live on forever."

I had no response for Paul, I just sat in silence. After a few minutes the old man stood up to say " I see you're in great thought my friend so I'll leave you for now." As Paul walked away he turned to me and said these words, " I hope you study the word my friend to find yourself approved by God Himself." The old man just turned and walked away to put up his tray. I didn't know what to think at this point, so I got up and put my tray away myself. I went back to my bunk and grabbed my Bible and started to read. As I was reading I came across scripture that read study to find yourself approved by God and not by men. This scripture blew my mind because the old man had just said similar words to me not so long ago. My reading I believe was just still that, reading at this point. Sure some scripture jumped out at me and I understood. In Matthew somewhere scripture reads something like this, " why do you look at the speck in your brothers eye when you cannot see the when you cannot see the plank in your own, judge lest you be judged and measured back onto you as you have judged. This scripture rang true in my mind because many of times I had either called someone out for their fault or mis/take while I was making a mis/take myself. Wow how true those words hit me at that moment. I quickly shut my Bible because I felt overwhelmed and started to cry. I guess the words had touched me so deeply I felt remorseful of my judgment towards other peoples mis/takes or faults.

I just laid there on my bunk thinking about what the old wise man had been saying to me. The word "study" kept crossing my mind and left me restless and hungry. It wasn't a physical hunger but a spiritual and mental hunger. So I grabbed my Bible and once again let the pages roll open to where they may. I felt like I was just jumping around in the Bible with no direction or guidance. I just kept reading hoping I would get more understanding of what it really meant so I could apply it to my life.

Once again chow, chow time came over the loud speakers, I got up off my bunk and went to the line. I made it to the door and grabbed my bag and juice, like usual I went back to my bunk and sat down. While I was eating I was expecting Paul to show up, but he never did to eat lunch with me. I guess I was a little disappointed because he seemed so wise to me. I finished my lunch drank my juice and then I grabbed my Bible from under my pillow and started to lay back on my bunk. Then I heard my name "David" I knew that deep voice belonged to Paul. He walked up and said, " I see you have your Bible in hand." I responded by saying, " yes Sir." Paul just smiled at me and asked to sit, I told him I wouldn't mind.

He began the conversation by asking me, " have you read and learned anything from scripture since we had talked?" I answered quickly by saying yes and proceeded to tell him about the plank in my eye and the speck in my brotherens eye. Paul looked at me and smiled as he told me that my plank was whittling to a speck. This time it was me that laughed and it felt good since I had been crying. Paul began to laugh with me with that soft twinkle in his eyes. There we were like tow old friends laughing like we were watching a comedy on T.V. or something. I believe we laughed for a few minutes before we came back to reality.

Just then the old man just turned and looked at me. He had a question and I could see it in his eyes. Sure enough he opened his mouth and there it came " has your name appeared upon the work list yet?" Trusties never get a job right away you sit a week or two for whatever reason. I answered Paul with just a no. He then told me his name was finally on the list. I didn't even get a chance to ask the question, Paul just said, " I work over night in the kitchen." Paul and myself just sat there on my bunk and talked for hours passing the time. I would tell him something about myself and then he would tell me something about himself. We would exchange questions back and forth. He then laughed at me after a few questions so I asked Paul what was so funny. Paul just chuckled as he said, " David why do you ask me the same question I ask you?" I answered quickly with Paul I am not sure! He laughed some more and with a slight pause he said, " do you have any originality about yourself?" After a slight pause myself I answered, " yes I sure do!" Paul jumped right in and said, " what might that be then." without a thought I said, ' I am a poet, and I was published in a contest." The book is in the National Library of Congress in Washington DC." Paul looked at me with a smile and said, "really." I responded by saying " yes and the book title is A Question of Balance, with my poem on page sixty eight second column last poem."

Paul jumped in to say, " The Blues! " I was shocked because that was the title of my poem. Before I could say a word Paul started to recite my poem.

"The Blues
Nobody knows why we get the blues,
Because we never leave any clues,
Sometimes it's love,
Sometimes it's hate,
It even happens on a date,
Nobody knows why,
But I really could die!"

I know I must have looked shocked by what the old man said, " David I can't believe I sit here with a great poet in a county jail and didn't know it." I looked at Paul and said, " I'm not sure about great but I do write to pass the time when I'm not working. Paul shook his head at me like if he was in disbelief of what I had said. Paul went about telling me that so many people never achieve their dreams because they give up on themselves. Those words rang true in my ears and made me think, I could tell the old man was going to say something but I beat him to it. Paul your right I gave up on myself many years ago after I had three poems published. Paul asked me why I gave up because I seemed so talented to him. I began to tell him the story that I never won a contest and two books I tried to have published were stolen from me. Paul didn't give me a pity party or say that he understood, he just looked at me and said these words! " What a waste of God given talent, just listen to the words." "Nobody knows why we get the blues!" He stopped and then said this, " God knows why and no one here on earth does because we all get the blues." If we could figure that out we probably wouldn't get the blues, well depressed we really call it."

Chow, chow time came over the loud speakers at this time. The old man looked at me as if to say dinner is here and we should get some, so I put my Bible under my pillow in its spot. In all that time we hardly discussed the Bible and it's true meaning. Paul and myself stood there in the line for our dinner for a few minutes before we made it to the door. I was really getting tired of the food but I would eat it anyway. Paul asked if he could sit with me some more. So there we sat an old man and a young man eating and talking, it was like we had been forever. I loved it when Paul would turn his head to face me, that usually meant words of wisdom were on their way. Sure enough upon that thought the old man turned his head and looked at me. The question just came out like lava from a volcano, " do you know what forgiveness is David." It took me a minute or so of thought before I responded. Paul I believe forgiveness is a thought process of a human being letting go of bad words or actions by someone else towards them. This helps the person that had to forgive the other person to still have kind words or actions towards the offender. The old man just smiled at me with these words to follow, " my son you are growing in the mighty Word of God." I was going to ask him a question but like if he knew he said, " David the more you read Gods word especially the New Testament your eyes will be opened, I had no response for his words seemed so pure. I suppose he felt this from me and said, " David I am going to leave you now but as I do you should read Second Corinthians chapter three.

Chapter Five

That night as I laid in my bunk I started to read my Bible. It's strange now that I really think about it so many years later, that Paul and myself had such a great time in a place where fun wouldn't even seem possible to anyone else. I did read the scripture that night, Second Corinthians chapter three. This scripture is about how when one turns to the New Testament a veil is lifted from ones' mind and heart. (The heart being your soul and the veil being hate.) Because when one turns to the Lord Jesus Christ and by the Holy Spirit, He gives us a better understanding about life. This is what I got out of it any way, by what Jesus and the Holy Spirit was showing me that night. I closed my Bible and put it under my pillow and went to sleep. I must have been at so much peace that night I never heard lock down announced or even woke up at all that I could recall.

The next morning came with the same announcement like always chow, chow time. So I got off my bunk and got in line. I received my breakfast knowing Paul wouldn't be there to sit with me. He was still working in the kitchen because the overnight shift made the lunches and breakfast for the whole jail. I ate my breakfast and put my tray away to go back to my bunk to pull my Bible out for the pages to unroll to where they may. I began to read as always just trying to understand but I guess my mind and soul wasn't into it that morning so I put my Bible away. I was frustrated and angry as I was reading, it just seemed like nothing I was making any sense. So I decided the best thing to do was to lay back down and sleep. I was woke up by the night shift coming back in from work, I only looked up for a minute to go right back to sleep. After the night shift came back in and showered we were put into lock down for a head count. We didn't have to stay in lock down for very long because shift change for the officers shift change was already in progress.

After lock down I felt a nudge at my bunk as I heard my name. In that deep loving voice Paul had. I looked up and there he stood, smiling from ear to ear. I didn't smile back at all I probably had a frown on my face. Paul asked me what was wrong, as I said with what was an unhappy voice. " I tried to read my Bible this morning after chow and I wasn't understanding so I shut it and went back to sleep."

I then told Paul I felt like I didn't have any guidance or direction in my study of the Bible. Paul looked at me with a sad look in his eyes. No twinkle in them at all as he stared at me blankly. I said " I am sorry Paul please forgive me I know you have helped me but you're not always here." Paul responded by saying, " look here my child I understand what you mean." Paul then asked me if he could sit. I said sure, I just knew I loved that old man. So I took my blanket off and swung my legs off my bed and let Paul sit down.

Paul sat down and said did you read Second Corinthians chapter three last night? I answered with my yes. Paul asked me what it meant to me, so I told him that I believe that God was telling me that if I turned to Jesus who is God in the flesh I would see more clearly. Paul just sat there as if he was waiting to hear more, he did have a smile on his face and that twinkle in his eyes. Then Paul spoke to me and said,

" what else do you have to say?" I looked back at Paul smiling with these words. Paul I figured you would have something to say some words of wisdom or something. Paul answered me back by saying, " you had the words of wisdom and I was just going to listen to them."

I sat there for a moment and then I said. Well Paul I believe you're wiser then me and I count on that. Paul began to chuckle at me and said, " David you are growing tall and strong and soon you will be wiser than ever before." We talked a little while longer and laughed at times. Paul once again excused himself politely saying he wanted to rest. We said our goodbyes and he went his way. I knew my time would be coming soon to be on the work list. I got off my bunk to go and look, sure enough there was my name on the over-night schedule for the kitchen. I was excited because I just knew that Paul and myself would work great with each other.

I went back to my bunk to read my Bible, as I was getting closer I saw a piece of paper on it. I thought dear Lord Jesus what could this be. There laid a correspondence Bible study and on the inside the study was on the book of Matthew. I sat down on my bunk and just thought that Paul had left it there. I began the study as it directed me on which chapters to read. I finished reading the study and then started to answer the questions at the end of the study, as I had to write an essay of what it had meant to me as well.

Chow, chow time was called out again into the dorm lunch was going to be served. My stomach jumped because I knew that my old wise friend would appear soon. Sure enough I grabbed my lunch when I made it to the door, then I turned and walked to my bunk. As I passed by Paul in the line he said he would come and sit with me. He showed up with lunch and juice in hand and a smile on his face. Before he could take a seat on my bunk I thanked him for the

Bible study I found on my bunk. Paul sat down beside me and said, " we have only begun to study the Bible together and there was no need to thank him." I said " no Paul I mean the correspondence Bible study you had left me on my bunk. This was the first time I saw a real lost look in his eyes. Paul then replied " I didn't leave you any Bible study on your bunk.

I pulled my Bible out from under its place and removed the study from the book of Matthew to show it to him. Paul then told me that he didn't leave me the study on my bunk. I was in awe with no words to say to him. Paul jumped in and said, " God must have heard you tell me you didn't feel like you had all the guidance or direction you needed." I thought to myself for awhile wondering who might have left the study for me. I suppose it was pretty obvious to Paul because he begun to speak to me. " David look at all these guys in here with us." I started to look around the dorm at all the guys and turned back to look at the old man. Paul looked me in the eyes and begun to speak those words of wisdom to me again. My ears perked up as he said this to me, " These other sixty six guys may not look like or act like God uses them but God is in all of them." " Whether bound to Christ or free of Christ, He is all in all. He is listening even when they are not, He is faithful even when they are not." I looked at Paul and once again my facial expressions must have said I am lost.

Paul then said, " a bound person is a person that believes Jesus was and is God in the flesh and unbound is just a person that has just not believed yet. My eyes and face must have lit up once again, I could tell by Paul's' words right after that. " David I can see that you have come to believe in Jesus as I can see it on you." " What do you mean Paul?" I asked. Paul went silent for just a minute or so, like he was in deep thought. " David when I speak scripture to you, I see your eyes and face light up like a candle. Do you see that happen to me my dear friend as you speak scripture to me." I thought for a second or two before I let out my trembling yes out.

The conversation took on a little lighter of a subject not that we wanted it to go like that. I guess we both just needed to take a break from the spiritual side of us. Paul began to tell me of a cat he had long ago and how he missed its loving nature. I then told him of several that I had at one time or another. Just then it dawned on me that I was to start in the kitchen on his shift. When I began to tell Paul about my good fortune his eyes lit up like a little child on Christmas morning. Just as I was going to tell him that I knew I would like to work along side of him without a doubt. Paul stood up to stretch, we had been sitting there for a long time. Paul spoke saying, " we had about an hour and a half before dinner chow and wanted to rest. I told him ok, and he said I'll see you for chow my dear friend.

I laid back on my bunk and began to read my Bible some more. I believe I was changing by the day as my mind had less negative thoughts. I found myself not thinking about my past mis/takes as often. I even started having joyful memories again from my childhood to that day talking with Paul in jail. I shut my Bible because I knew chow time wasn't far off, putting my Bible under my pillow I figured I would rest awhile.

Sure enough about thirty minutes went by and chow, chow time was announced over the loud speakers. I went to the line and waited my turn for my tray. As I stood there I felt a nudge from behind and it was Paul. He said, " my dear friend may I sit with you?" I said sure that I wouldn't mind the company.

We got our trays and headed back to my bunk to eat, for a few minutes we were silent as we ate. Paul begun to talk just too break the silence I believe, " David " Paul said with a joy in his voice. " I am an old man in life, I had so much but now so little." He also said, that he was happy and successful in all he had done as well.

I stopped the old man just then to ask him what he meant. " Oh my child, I had everything a man could ever want at one time. I had a business that made lots of money, a wife and children. " What happened Paul?" I asked him. He paused for what seemed to be forever in my mind as I could see he was holding back tears.

Paul then begun to speak in that deep, loving and gentle voice he had." Well I am seventy five now so I guess it's been thirty years ago. Yeah I was forty five and my wife and I had everything a happy couple would ever need. It was a month before Christmas and my wife went out shopping, oh how Nancy loved to shop." Paul stopped to laugh, I believe he laughed so he wouldn't have started to cry. The Paul started to tell me his story some more.

"Oh yes, Nancy was a giving, loving person as she would shop for our children. Nancy would also would buy gifts for less fortunate people, we knew as personally. I didn't ever mind because we knew how blessed we were by the grace of God and we really had so much. Nancy would also find local homeless people and bless them as well, because we knew and understood they were God's children, just like anybody else.

I could see the tears welling up in those soft grey eyes of his. I spoke up and asked him if he was ok. Paul answered with a quick yes, and proceeded to talk. " Nancy had finished her shopping and was headed for home when my whole world changed. From what I was told that at a red light she was robbed and killed for all she had in the car." I couldn't believe what Paul was saying at this time. He got chocked up at this time by the sound of his voice, as I just stared in disbelief.

Paul recovered quickly to my amazement as he apologized to me. I told him there was no need to be sorry to me. Paul began to tell his story. My children at the time were off in collage so they worked even harder to take their minds off Nancy's' death. I could tell Paul had a struggle within himself at this point. He went silent for a few minutes again with his hands holding his head.

I broke the silence again asking Paul if he would forgive me because I wanted to rest before work. Paul answered me saying forgiveness was not needed between us. He knew that we should rest to be productive later at work, for it is a privilege in jail. We said our good bys' and we loved one another, what love is greater then brotherly love. I started to read more scripture as it was seeming to sooth my soul as I studied and studied.

Chapter Six

The work hour had appeared quickly to me, so I got off my bunk and headed towards the door where several other guys were waiting. With some small greetings and a few hellos we just stood there. Paul showed up a couple minutes later a little groggy he said his hellos. The correction officers unlocked the dorm door to let us out to stand in the center of the dorms. Other inmates were to come out of their dorms so we all could get budged.

I guess to keep peace and order this is how the jail found it to be the easiest way. After the correction officers did their head count and handed out badges they lead us to the kitchen. Inside the kitchen the staff members assigned everyone a job. I got appointed to bag lunches as Paul was already making sandwiches. I was working alongside a guy that already had been bagging lunches, so he taught me. I would have rather been working by Paul but neither of us were in control over that.

My job consisted of putting two sandwiches in a lunch bag with two cookies, peanut butter, jelly packets and a small bag of chips. We had to make three thousand of these from ten thirty until almost two in the morning. We then had to break all of that down to prepare to serve the breakfast trays. The whole jail had to be served by five o' clock A.M.

It was very interesting to me how fast this would all happen. For all of these guys to come together and make this happen was truly amazing in my eyes. Individually we might have messed up on the outside to get us in that jail, but in that kitchen we were a team. We cleaned the kitchen to be sent back to our dorms by six o' clock. It amazes me to this day when I think about how this handful of misfits made three thousand launches and fixed three thousand breakfast trays and cleaned that kitchen in less then seven hours. Talking about moving a mountain, I believe the fifteen of us did this every night.

Back inside the dorm, Paul and myself had agreed after lock down for head count and some rest we would get together and talk. I took my shower and headed to my bunk to find another Bible study. I received one back and got a new one for I was doing extremely well. I rested for about two hours to wake up to start the new study. I was really getting into all the spiritual blessings and messages I was receiving by the instructor, Paul and the ministers that held church services where the visitation rooms where above the dorms.

I'm not sure how long it had been but I was engrossed in my study and I didn't realize Paul had walked up. He asked if he could sit and I told him yes. Paul asked me how it was going and I told him I thought it was going very well. The old man just said with a smile that's good and patted me on the back. I was thinking to myself he was going to finish his story at this time.

Paul smiled at me with those big grey eyes as if to say he was proud of me for whatever reason. He then spoke in that loving voice he owned. " David life can be hard at times, but if you have understanding knowledge and wisdom your life can and will become easier for you and your own mind." The old man also proceeded to tell me how ones' own mind is the owners own world or creation. Once again I must have had that I am lost look in my eyes.

Paul took a great pause for a few minutes from speaking to me. He begun to speak to me like I was his child. " Son, let me tell you after Nancy had died I was lost, spinning out of control. I had begun to drink all the time and had no positive thoughts about life anymore. My business started losing money and I started to lose hope in everything. I then asked Paul what happened to help him.

Paul chuckled like always and said he changed his life the only way he knew how. I started going to Bible studies with a friend of mine, and arose from the ashes of his negative thinking. Paul was a very wise man as I could tell by his words and stories. Once again the old man told me that he was tired and needed some rest for awhile. So Paul stood up, as he stretched his body we said our good byes and I love yous.

I took my Bible back in hand and laid back on my bunk, once again I started to read what the Bible study instructed me to read. All of the noise and chaos seemed to be drowned out by the study I was pressing into. The Bible studies were starting to get easier and easier for me at this time. I wasn't having to reread the scriptures as many times like before to find the answers. Before long I was writing my essay on what I thought the scriptures were about. The Holy Bible is for a healthy spiritual life with God and a better life between others and yourself, even though it isn't always perfect or easy.

Just then chow, chow time came over those loud speakers like always. I climbed off my bunk and got in line for my bag and juice. I finally made it to the door and received my lunch, on my way back I didn't see Paul at all. I sat down hopping he would appear so we could talk and share some laughs. As I sat there in my own silence eating my lunch my thoughts started to torment me. They were negative with the thoughts that I would never get out of this cold damp Hades. The old mans words came to mind right then, " your mind is your world or creation." So I managed to get hold of my thoughts and pretended I was on a beach somewhere listening to the roaring waves crashing. To my surprise my thoughts soothed me, they made me laugh and feel good inside my mind.

Just then Paul showed up and said me what was so funny. I told him about the great attack of negativity and how I beat those heeish thoughts. Paul and I began to laugh some more uncontrollable like we had just heard the funniest joke ever. We finally stopped our childish laughs after what had seemed to be forever to me.

Paul then asked me if he could sit so we could talk like always I told him that I wouldn't mind at all. As he took his place beside me on my bunk I could see it in his eyes he had something to say. Paul began to speak words of wisdom like always, " David this is what I've been telling you this whole time we have been talking. So many people are trapped and entombed in their own low self-esteem and negative thoughts, they believe they can't be successful." I replied to Paul with these words that I'll never forget. " Paul, so many people struggle just to make enough money to pay their bills and have what they need. So how are they to feel successful in their lives as they work for someone who could careless about if their needs are met?"

I imagine Paul went into great thought upon his silence from my statement. Then there it came all at once like lava from a volcano. " David when we find ourselves serving an ungrateful master we should not work with mediocrity we should do more then they ask. This brings us back to the scripture, " whom so ever compels you to go with them one mile go another and another and more if needed. The mediocre worker never goes above and beyond what their boss ask them to do. They only do the bare minimum of what they have been asked to do. People who do this don't want to feel cheated in what they have received for what they have done which leaves themselves cheated. To go above and beyond in all you do has to come from your own self initiative by your own positive thoughts."He also said these words to me, " David do you remember who was the speaker of those words in the Bible." I answered quickly with my yes and said Jesus. The old man then told me that God would be in debt for all the extra work if I wouldn't hold a debt in my heart towards the person I was serving. These words of wisdom started to make sense to me by all the scripture I had been studying this whole time. The Lords prayer in Matthew chapter six came to mind ; Forgive us as we forgive our debtors pooped out at me from that prayer. I know in my heart and mind that I had delivered more sweet then the money I had received many of times in my life.

With this thought I asked Paul if these scriptures applied to my past. Paul answered me quickly with his words. God is a forgiving God and upon our forgiveness and self-forgiveness he could restore our lives. He also told me and reminded me that this all happens in Gods own timing and not in ours. I just knew how true those words were because I had read similar words in scripture within my studies. I could see the old man was getting tired in his eyes. This didn't stop him by any means, his words of wisdom just kept pouring out like water from a deep well. I just hung onto his words with my undivided attention. He made a great teacher and I was the student. He stopped at one point to ask me if I knew who Solomon was in the Bible. I answered Paul by saying I believed he was a great king full of Gods' wisdom.

Paul was smiling from ear to ear with his twinkling eyes, Paul said to me " yes." He also told me that anyone could obtain and surpass the wisdom of Solomon if they would lose the doubt of it in their mind. I must have had a puzzled look in my eyes to Paul. He then told me that Solomon was wise but also stopped following Gods' instructions and that's why he fell. He then told me he could tell my wisdom was coming from Gods' Holy Spirit and God would lead me to my own success. All I had to do is take counsel to these five basic laws that God put into place since the beginning of time.

I then asked Paul to explain what he meant by this, he told me that I already had the answers inside of myself. My response was a little short when I said I didn't understand. Paul just chuckled like he always did at my foolishness. Paul then spoke these last few words before he excused himself. " You are growing tall and wise and the fruits of the land will soon be yours." He stood up and stretched and we said our good byes' and I love yous' and he walked off.

Chapter Seven

The days had turned into weeks and the weeks had turned into months, while Paul and myself would sit and talk. Between the Bible studies and our talks I hadn't realized that five months had passed us by. The funny part about it is in all this time Paul and I never asked one another what we had done to be put in jail. I laughed at my thought and Paul asked me what was so funny. I told him my thought and he laughed with me. Paul turned to me and this usually meant words of wisdom were coming. To my surprise this is what he said instead. David he spoke in that deep loving voice, let me tell you the rest of my story if you don't mind.

"Nancy had died and I recovered from my negative thoughts and retained my business, I was successful by the grace, mercy and love of God. I still thank Him to this day even right here in jail with you my dear friend. So I did the one last thing I knew I could do Paul said to me, I sold my business and gave my hardest of workers a good share as I didn't need much. I then moved away from my home town and started a new mission, I became a rag picker of sorts I guess." I stopped Paul by saying, " you collected junk Paul why would you do that? Paul didn't you have more then you needed?" Paul just laughed as it boomed through the dorm like always when he laughed real hard and loud at me.

Paul then replied by saying, " I became a rag picker of the human kind. I sought out people who thought they were worthless, unsaveable, unreachable and incapable of having a successful life. As I would find them one by one I would tell them my story and the five secrets to success." I stopped Paul by saying, " didn't that take forever and how did you hold their attention that long." Paul just laughed again as he smiled at me and said, " oh my silly child I had written it and typed it and made copies of it. I handed it out one by one after I convinced the people two still cared, God in heaven and me here on the earth with them.

I asked Paul if his message was successful and he replied that he was sure it was. He smiled and said to me he knew it helped at least one. I asked Paul how he knew it had helped at least one, he replied that the one it had help was himself and he was sure it had helped others. How are you certain it helped others I asked Paul.. His answer came quickly as he said, " more then once someone would stop him in the street and thanked him for the book and that was more then money could ever pay."

Paul finally told me what had got him put in jail, I prayed to God and asked him to let me help one last person before I died. I looked at Paul in disbelief and said you prayed to go to jail. David Paul replied " I didn't know I was going to end up in jail it just seemed to happen and then there you were right in her with me searching for help." Then Paul asked me if I had found the five laws of God. I told him that I was still searching for them in my studies. In all of my studies that I had received back my test scores were ninety percent or better and the lowest one was eighty five percent. Paul then turned to me with a smile on his face and said. " The five laws are these, count your blessings of how your body functions to move breath see and hear.

Proclaim your reality of how God made you. Go all the miles you can for everyone you can. Use your power of choice more wisely towards other people and yourself. And there is one more law that supersedes the other four laws, the law of love. Do all things out of love for God all others and of course yourself." Paul then said he would talk to me soon as he needed to go lay down and rest for he was very tired.

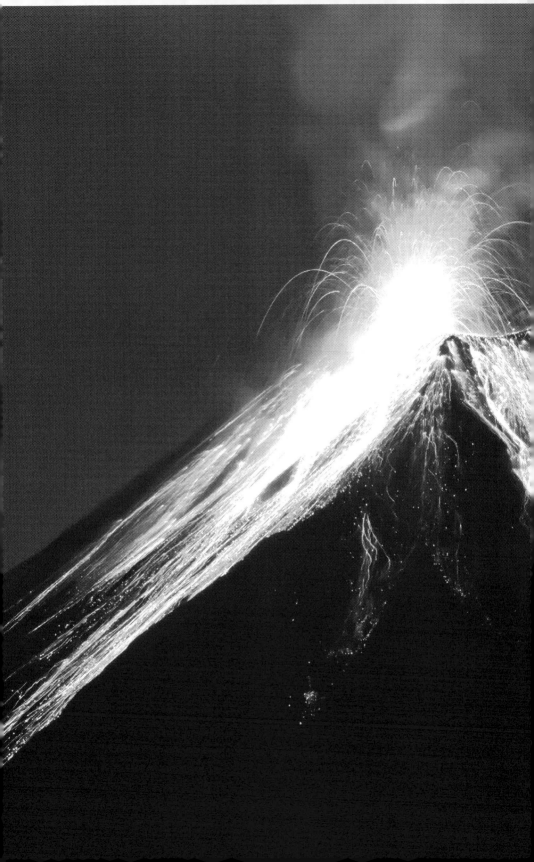

From The Ashes of Negative Thinking

A testimony to God my Lord and Savior Jesus Christ. By His love, grace and mercy I had a great experience to write and be blessed by this great message by God. By His Holy Spirit I came to understand more about life and His way of life for myself.

Now this brings me to this part of this great and message and gift from God: to you: I pray you fulfill this mission you will be set out to do in life and for your life.

This great and powerful message will not do anything for you unless you really apply it and put it to work. It can not and will not ever move you, unless you move and grow with the message.

So you get challenged today as you start your mission by God Himself and your own self for a new life.

There is a cost, but nothing you can not pay. What this will cost you is about thirty minutes of your time every night. Not much of a cost if you would like to achieve it's rare rewards.

First look at the date this night and know that you begin your mission on giving yourself and the rest of the world a new you.

Now mark this date on your calendar and count one hundred

days forward and mark that date. Then read this message just before you go to sleep and let it slip into your subconscious mind that never sleeps. Do not let one little thing stop you from reading the whole book in these one hundred days, and sleep in peace as you do it.

Then do one more thing when you finish your hundred day mission. Find someone like your old-self and give him/her two things Gods love and the book.

I sit and think as a human, as a writer and as an individual that had much and now so little. I think back over time and the choices I've made, living with no self-doubt or regrets of my mis/takes in my life. Like if to say my life has been a movie or a play.

I know today that it is true that our lives or individual lives is just that, a movie or a play rehearsed daily for the better or worse of what we make it. You are the only one that has control over your mis/takes or perfect/takes like you rehearsed it a million times before. Reading and living your life every-day perfectly is impossible but surely not impossibly lived. A journey lived and ventured beyond the past is very possible and important so one can live in the fullness of positive thoughts everyday.

I had to learn in the hardest of ways the simplicity of an easier life I have always desired to live. I have obtained this easier, better and simpler life by the word of God. The belief of "I" doesn't even equal self. "I" is encircled and becomes a "you" with a divine wisdom by the Holy Spirit, when you open your mind and soul to understand more than "Self" or "Self-righteousness."

Humanity in all the centuries that have passed has tried to understand all the possibilities and different theories of the how's, why's, when's and what's of who we are. We, us and you, can not exist without an "I." God said " I am and He made humanity or humans in His image and onto the likeness of Himself." God in His image means God must of had a Self Image. So, If He could see Self wouldn't that mean He saw "Himself" as a Man as He saw us as Humans? Wouldn't this make us a part of Him?

Now with this thought or reasoning inside your mind, which is your world or creation. Stop and think of the world you would create for yourself and all the people around you. I found that when I took self out of my mind and added others to it, life started to become something new for myself. I started noticing that others are seeing me in a different way. Sure some might say I am just a do gooder, a person wanting recognition for something I did. This would be a wrong thought by them I would have to say!

I have found a new happiness again in life, like when I was a child before I lost it's innocence. I am trying and never will stop trying to spread this new happiness I have found inside my own mind or world. Happiness is achieved in ones own mind and knots what's outside the mind. Your mind and thoughts of others can only lead you to a better mental perception of your-self and others around you by actions, words and belief in humanity and how we should really act towards each other and ones self. The thought of this, the practice of this has brought me to a greater and better understanding of other people, my-self and life by it's self. these thoughts brought into my life through other peoples words and actions helped me to realize these words of I can instead of the words I can't. This has now changed my own life.

You might be thinking to yourself right now, how can I change my-self for the better? I hope you let that negative thought go and think positively that you can change and make a difference in life and your life. Your mind only works in two ways and you have control over your thoughts. Whether your thoughts are about others, yourself or life by it's self. Your positive or negative thoughts lead you by your eye sight to the physical realm of what you see to be real or manifested. This is to think it, say it and believe it to be real and it will be just that a positive or negative out come. This meaning anything positive is for you and anything negative is against you. Your positive thoughts will lead you to a better life, if you let it. Just train your brain to be positive instead of negative, I have found this to be true in my own life.

Let's just say you have a friend that has negative thoughts about their own life and life it's self. You like your friend, so you encourage your friend with more positive thoughts about their self and some how it sinks in and changes the way they think about themselves, others and life by it's self. Now your friend is in a better place of his or her own mind. With more positive thoughts and a better out-look on their own life and others around them, the positive thoughts then reach beyond you by your friend to help others that you may never know or get to meet. Now your positive thoughts and actions are reaching out to touch and help other people around you even though you might not see it happening. Your positive thinking is helping this take place without your-self ever taking place in it. Now this is a positive and selfless act in life. This is success and happiness that is within your reach by thinking, speaking and doing more positive things for others and yourself.

The human mind controls it's physical surroundings starting with the human body. This gives you the capabilities to move, breath, see and hear. You should always be grateful and thankful of this happening, which is all done inside your brain even if you don't realize it. Now as these thoughts are playing a bigger part in your every-day life, your rarity, uniqueness an individuality should shine through from the inside. No two people are the same although we may have some similarities or even a twin brother or sister, but the way we think, act and talk separates us to our individuality. I believe God placed this with-in us all, He made us from the beginning of time. I also believe by my research of the Holy Bible and my studies in scriptures that God truly intended us to be like Him. He wants us to be kind, loving, helpful and positive. This to my understanding and knowledge is Him needing us to help Him rebuild a broken world of people in disarray, disbelief that they are loved by God Himself.

These thoughts and reasoning penetrated my mind, just as they should penetrate yours. Nothing over-rules the power of love, kindness and positive thinking for these can change a dark defeated mind into a bright, positive ever-changing mind for all who wish to do so. Daily application and dedication to this is needed for your-self not to go back to the " old you " of negative thoughts and the words I can't. Now as time goes on and you begin your " new life. " The life that had been intended for you since your " first birth " you have been reborn. With your rebirth and newness of " your-mind " all good things are possible and are there within your reach. Life and the things of it can be a challenge " you " can defeat them all with the newness of life and your new mind-set of " I still can. " Did you ever think as a child growing into who you are that you should be doing more with " your-self? " I have no doubt that the possibilities of this running through your brain as these thoughts have been in my own mind as well.

I had to dig deep inside of myself when I felt the pricks, stings and hard-ships of life. I found myself homeless, broke and desperate for a change. I started reaching out to humanity out to humanity in many ways not for a hand out hand up or anything else but understanding, knowledge and wisdom. I found this in reading, listening and becoming more open minded and hearted.. The word of God was the biggest part of my new beginning in the renewing of my mind. I started reading other books and finding similar messages that related to God and His mighty words of truth! Not knowing how to handle all of these positive messages coming together a great attack of negativity moved into my mind. I realized the attack and fought it off by pressing forth in the most positive ways. The more I experienced good and better things happening to me, the more I prayed and thought positive.

From the ashes of negative thoughts replaced by positive thoughts the mind comes alive with new hopes and dreams and desires of achievement. To achieve anything your mind has to be changed by you to put into action the things you need to do. The first thing you can do is start small and let your first action grow into bigger actions to accomplish the goal you started with your first small action. even if your first action was just a list of the things needed to be done by you to accomplish the goal. Never become disappointed in setbacks, struggles and even in areas of the goal where there seems to be no progress. If you let this happen you become what you were before, just another person living what we all did before and it's a living death. This meaning you have a life with no meaning or purpose or drive to improve other peoples lives or your own. I feel it's better to be dead then to live as I did before " a living death."

I find life in other people now as I find life inside myself. To figure out life is to understand your purpose in life and help others do the same for themselves. These are all positive things and have to start with-in your own mind. Never give up the present things for the things of the past that are gone which are dead. The reasons of having the things of the present is they are more and better things that you need at this time, so you can learn to give and receive more. I believe this is true by my reasoning and thought processes of I make better and wiser choices of how I treat others by my more positive thoughts and this gives me more to help others with. By my words, actions and the little things I could give away when I started this journey, a journey of just wanting to write my own self help book. I am now watching my self act help so many others around me. Now I really understand how great selfless acts of just a few more positive words and actions can really help so many others.

To forgive yourself and others that may seem to be against you is to make the statement to yourself. If you truly forgive others as we should bitter words seem to fade away in the company of others I see this everyday in my own life. Self forgiveness is important for you to get past your mis/takes in life, so others can forgive themselves as God has forgiven us. Our failures and transgressions should never hold ourselves back from our full potential of how we should live. We should live in love for our neighbor, ourselves and all others even if we never meet them. I have found that waking up in love for myself, all others and God is a miracle that God has given us each day we have life. The importance of us to acknowledge this is to bring peace, love and joy into other peoples lives.

With the forgiveness of others when we believe that they might have been trying to hurt us, we come to understand others by remaining in their lives. I have found the more I see humanity with my eyes of forgiveness no-matter the words or actions the bad moments don't seem so bad or don't last so long. No one is perfect and when fault comes forth with this new mind set of forgiveness of self and others the fault seems not to be faulty at all. The word of God says, that you should forgive anyone seventy time seventy and more if needed. A slap to one cheek turn the other before responding back in the same manner. Humanity has to be built and re-built upon forgiveness and love.

The power of love changes everything in life, as I see my life change year by year. The love of God moves and keeps moving through everyone around me. This power leaves me in awe most days and more so as I see it from a distance. I see acts of kindness take place between two other people and I realize more and more humanity still has hope and faith in their selves and others. I feel so blessed to the thoughts of life is special to me by other people even when the actions don't touch my life, I let it touch my life by my mind set of I still have faith and hope in humanity and myself.

The bond of forgiveness between everyone in life keeps togetherness in reach when we really apply this to our lives. We become more able to help others and get help from others when we have forgiveness in our hearts and minds. Our self pride fades and makes it easier to give and receive as we all need help in life because troubles come and go for everyone. The love, grace, mercy and forgiveness of God to us left no-one out just by believing He has done this for you. With this thought it became easier to forgive myself for my mis/takes that I have made though out my life. With this concept in my mind everyday I just keep moving forward in life with no self-doubt or regrets when of my everyday life even when I make a mis/take. This makes all of my days easier to reflect on and learn from as I remember them.

Now with your new mind set of self-forgiveness you should

love yourself again like you did as a child. With this new love you should find it easier to love all others as I have found this to be true in my life. Hatred should fade away from your mind with this new found love given to us by God Himself and by no other force in the universe. These thoughts of truth came into my life as I studied the Holy Bible and came to understand God as Jesus Christ. In the New Testament Jesus who is God is teaching us how to love ourselves, all other people when we open our souls and minds to love and forgiveness.

This great message of self forgiveness helps free your mind of negativity and the condemning feelings life can sway you to believe. With your new free mind and positive mental activity you can help change the world of people around you. For I believe this is helping God and ourselves to restore us and His world back to the paradise and Garden of Eden that He intended us to live in from the beginning of time. So as you apply Gods love and forgiveness to your life with daily application and dedication, you should see great changes in your everyday life.

Gods' grace, mercy and love is a gift to all people by Jesus Christ. This gift is not earned by anything we do, it is just that a gift of love from God Himself. I feel compelled by Gods' Holy Spirit of love to share this great gift and message with all of humanity. The thoughts of humanity not understanding this great gift to all compels me even more to ask the questions. Who doesn't deserve this great gift to all of us? By His word God said, " He is all in all," so if He is all in all who is left out? Are you left out? Are your children left out? Is your neighbor left out? How can anyone be left out of the word all? Shouldn't we all be lifting each-other up to improve all of humanity?

I have found that when I ask people if they have faith or some kind of belief in God most say yes. So what are we really suppose to be doing with our faith? We should be sharing it with everyone. I do understand that there is some resistance in the world, but should this prevent us from doing what God has sent us into the world to do? He sent us into the world to share our faith by His grace, mercy and love.

Your deeds should be done in love for humanity never concerning yourself with what you might get out of it. Just compensation might not always come at time of service, but just payment could come at anytime for past, present or future labor you may perform or had preformed. Why consider or hold anyone human in debt for anything you have done for them. I believe that when you do all things out of love for God all others and yourself your life can change for the better. It seems that opportunity seeks us in so many different ways to bless others as it blesses us. Scripture reads " Whom so ever compels you to go with them one mile go another." This meaning to work for someone you should do all they ask and a little more no matter the pay with out feeling cheated for what you have received. Since I have applied this scripture to my life with daily application and dedication I have seen God do great things in my life. When I thought I would lack, I didn't. When I thought I wouldn't have, I had more. When I thought I would run out, I over flowed. My blessings seem to over flow my cup and it filled me with even more joy, peace and happiness with Gods love.

The word of God says: " He knows our hearts (soul) minds and thoughts. He asks us to step off into our prayer closets to spend to with Him. By His Holy Spirit I have a better understanding of what our prayer closet is. Our prayer closet is our minds and He wants us to spend time with Him there several times a day in your mind. Just for a few moments at a time to focus on what He needs us to do to make our days better for us. This will help you in having better days the more you do it. I know you might be thinking, how can I do this with my busy life but all your doing is making your life harder then it needs to be. I have a busy life myself but I take the time for Jesus everyday and find all the things I need are right there. You can have this in your life too just take the time in your mind and talk to Jesus as you need. With all of this in your mind with daily application you will find all the joy, happiness, forgiveness and love in your heart to make it through everyday in a positive way.

I remember times of struggles and asking God for help with them. God came upon me by His Holy Spirit and reminded me of the tools He bestowed upon us since the beginning of time so we could help ourselves. He gave us all talents, senses and the abilities to accomplish anything we set our minds to do. God gave us one more power so great that no other being in the universe has it or can use it. A power so great that nothing can stop it except you! He gave us the power to choose and the choices to make.

He gave us the power to think.
He gave us the power to give.
He gave us the power to laugh.
He gave us the power to create.
He gave us the power to will.
He gave us the power to speak.
He gave us the power to persevere.
He gave us the power to praise.
He gave us the power to act.
He gave us the power to heal.
He gave us the power to grow.

He gave us the power to live.

He gave us the power to love.

He gave us the power to work.

So you should give, instead of steal.

You should laugh, instead of cry.

You should create, instead of destroy.

You should love, instead of hate.

You should persevere. instead of quit.

You should praise, instead of curse.

You should act, instead of procrastinate.

You should heal, instead of wound.

You should grow, instead of rot.

You should live, instead of wanting to die.

You should be working on all of this for God all others and yourself to improve all of humanity. By now you should see your mis/takes were not Gods will at all, those were the times of your own will. Now with Gods better/takes for your life, your life can and will be better for you the little miniature god that God Himself entitled you to be. So now as you become the complete living being God intended you to be, count your blessings, be yourself, go all the miles you can go for every-one you can and use your power of choice more wisely.. These are the four greatest laws given to us by God for our growth to our own success and happiness.

There is one more law that supersedes the other four laws. The law of love, use this law to do all things for God all others and of course yourself. Then God can and will sit back in pride or sorrow of how you have acted towards humanity and yourself with your deeds. With these five laws applied to your life, if there is a debt let the debt fall on God. He is great to pay this debt with compound interest upon compound interest in His own time.

Now as God wants you to wipe away your tears you reborn child because like your first birth when He placed His hand upon you, you cried. We all cried! Now God wants you to stand up straight and lose your grave cloths that have bound you and go to work in your new found life with God Himself.

Chapter Eight

The next morning came and there was no announcements, no noise no nothing to wake me up. I must have been sleeping in so much peace the nudge I thought I was feeling didn't even work. Then in a deep loving voice I heard, " hey buddy wake up, you can't sleep here." I finally said, " Paul this isn't funny." I looked up to see an old man standing over me that looked like Paul." He said, " I am not Paul and you can't sleep in front of my business." I looked around and sure enough I wasn't in jail anymore, I picked up what I guess I was my own sleeping bag and pillow to walk away. As I got down the road I was confused of what was going on. I started to search my pockets to find something to help me understand. There in my back pocket I felt a piece of paper. I stopped at a bus stop bench lost and confused to sit down. I opened the paper to start to read it.

To my dearest friend David, I know you are lost and in your mind right now, clear your thoughts and take counsel to Gods' wisdom. As I have been your friend over the last several months and we came to know one another. You will have to understand and realize that our friendship had no boundaries, no matter where you were. Just know and realize that we had to part ways since you were finally set free of the prison of your own mind.

I also want you to remember our talks and come to understand that as much as you need God, He needs you as well. From one old rag picker to another young one, just know that it is better to live as it was my turn to die. I sat there and cried on that bus stop bench, but I felt warm on that cold winter day because I knew God and my old friend love me so.

Printed in the United States
By Bookmasters